AF428618

MAMA, I WANT TO FLY
BY: Claudene A. Graham

ISBN: 979-8-9858322-4-2
Imprint: Independently published

To order additional copies of this book,
Email:claudeneg14@gmail.com

DEDICATION

This book is dedicated with love to my children Alex & Imani, my nieces, nephews, and all the boys and girls who will read this book.

INTRODUCTION

Imani was so excited when her dad told her that she could be anything she wanted to be. So fascinated by the discovery, she told her friends at school what her dad said. It was electrifying as the children stated one after another what they wanted to be when they grow up.

MAMA, I WANT TO FLY

MAMA, I WANT TO FLY

Mama told Imani to get ready for breakfast.

Pancakes, eggs, and bacon are Imani's favorite.

"Pancakes, eggs, and bacon," Imani sang as she ran up the stairs for her dad. "Pancakes, eggs, and bacon."
"Pancakes, e…., daddy!"

Dad hugged Imani as they made their way to breakfast.

"Ok, Imani let's have breakfast so you can get to school on time." Mama said.

While they were having breakfast, Imani said, "Mama, I had a dream last night that I was flying to school."

"Did you?" Mama asked.
"Yea, I **flied** to school," Imani answered.

IMANI
BUTTER

Mama told Imani it's **FLEW**, not **flied**.
"**Flu**, that's when you are sick mama,"
Imani said.

Mama explained that **flu** is the sickness
and **flew** is the past tense of **fly**.
"It was last night, right?" Mama asked.

"Yes mama," Imani answered.

"So that's in the past," Mama responded.

"I flew, it sounds so weird, flew, flew," Imani said.

"I hope you were on time," her dad teased.

"Yea dad, I did not say I walked, I said I fly, I flew," Imani responded.

"Ok guys, you really must get going now, it's getting late, and we won't be flying," Mama joked.

"Dad, I want to be a superhero, a superwoman,

a police officer or maybe a principal."
"You don't have to wear a cape to be a superhero you know dad," Imani told her dad.

"I know Imani, and you do know you can be anything you want to be, right?" Dad asked Imani.

"For real dad, anything?" Imani asked.
"I can be a pilot?" she investigated.
"Well, sure you can be a pilot," Her dad responded.

"IMANI, ANYTHING YOU WANT! LET NO ONE TELL YOU OTHERWISE!" Dad emphasized.

"A nurse like you dad?" Imani inquired.

"Anything you want Imani," Dad declared
"COOL!" Imani exclaimed.

"Maybe I'll be a mechanic like mama and
work on monster trucks," Imani said.

"Anything, my daughter," Dad said.

"COOL!" Imani exclaimed.

At school, Imani asked her friends, "Do you know you can be anything you want to be when you grow up?"

"No, I cannot be a doctor, like James' dad I am not that smart," Jay said.

"Yea you can, my mama and daddy say you can, and if my mama and daddy say so it is so. Why don't you ask your daddy?"** Imani challenged.

Jay replied, "Ok, I will ask my daddy."

Listening to Imani saying it was possible to be anything they wanted to be, the children got all excited. They gathered around her to share what they wanted to be when they grow up.

"I want to be a teacher," Shania said.
"I will be a counselor," Reniece declared.
"My dream is to become a lawyer!" shouted Aiyana.

"I promise, I will be a nurse!" Ramone Yelled.

Mrs. S.
Book

"I aspire to be an engineer!" exclaimed Alex.
"I want to be a singerrr," Nickoy sang.
"I want to be a doctor too, but I will take care of babies like Zoe's mom.
A Pedi.
A Pedi.
A Pediatrician," Tiahna asserted.

ALEX

"I want to be a top chef," Nikki said.
"I am determined, to be a doctor," Kayon beamed.
"I intend to be an entrepreneur!" Jr. bellowed.
"I will be a pilot!" Jessica screamed.

"One day I will be the president of my country," Reniece declared.

"I WANT TO BE AN ASTRONAUT, AND A PILOT, AND A SUPER LADY. I CAN BE ANYTHING I WANT, MAMA, I WANT TO FLY!" Imani yelled.

PRESIDENT

About the Author

Claudene A. Graham is from the beautiful island of Jamaica. She is a nurse, author, and entrepreneur. Her books include REACH, SAY CHEESE IT'S A NEW DAY, and children's books WHEN I WAKE UP IN THE MORNING & MAMA, I WANT TO FLY. She is a mother of two children; Alex and Imani. Claudene is passionate about writing and bringing joy and laughter to others.